FIRECRAFT FOR THE FUTURE

SUSTAINABLE, ETHICAL & EFFICIENT FLAME

Firecraft for the Future: Sustainable, Ethical, and Efficient Flame
by Sulien Valentino Solovyov

ISBN: 978-1-989647-80-6 First published October 8, 2025
Toronto, Ontario

Publisher: The Evergreen Centre

Publisher's Cataloging-in-Publication Data

Solovyov, Sulien Valentino.
Firecraft for the Future : Sustainable, Ethical, and Efficient Flame / Sulien Valentino Solovyov. – First edition.

Summary: A comprehensive guide to mastering firecraft, focusing on the three pillars of ignition, lay, and efficiency, and providing techniques for sustainable methods, advanced fire structures, and Leave No Trace (LNT) principles for environmental stewardship.

Identifiers: ISBN 978-1-989647-80-6

Subjects: Firecraft. | Survival Skills. | Leave No Trace (LNT). | Fire Ethics. | Combustion Science. | Fuel Efficiency.

Classification: 796.5–dc23

Firecraft for the Future

Sustainable, Ethical, and Efficient Flame

by
Sulien Valentino Solovyov

A Note on the Series: Applied Vernacular

Welcome to the Chaptech / Applied Vernacular Series.

Chaptech / Applied Vernacular is the art of small, humble books that make knowledge tangible, practical, and joyfully human. Born from the earnest spirit of 1970s scout manuals, National Park pamphlets, mimeographed guides, and the enduring wisdom of the Appropriate Technology Library, it celebrates line drawings that verge on naïve, the charm of deliberately imperfect diagrams, and the tactile nature of hand-assembled care. It is instruction as intimacy, expertise as invitation, and the small book as a gateway to doing, making, and discovering.

In a world brimming with fleeting information, this collection is a quiet testament to enduring knowledge—the kind learned by hand, observed with patience, and proven by practice. Each book in this series is an invitation, a "first experiment" into a specific facet of the natural world or practical craft. We celebrate the Applied Vernacular: the language of hands-on wisdom, rooted in everyday experience and the ingenious solutions found in local living. These aren't exhaustive encyclopedias; they are humble field notes, concise guides designed to spark curiosity and equip you with foundational skills.

Within these pages, you'll find simple diagrams, prompts for observation, and space for your own notes and sketches. We believe the truest understanding comes from interaction—from trying, from watching, and from seeing how things truly work.

Carry this book with you. Let it get dog-eared, stained by soil, or marked with your own insights. Use it to deepen your connection to the world around you, to cultivate a quiet competence, and to rediscover the profound satisfaction that comes from knowledge in hand, and practice in heart.

Table of Contents:

Firecraft for the Future: Sustainable, Ethical, and Efficient Flame

THE THREE PILLARS OF MODERN FIRECRAFT

Ignition, Lay, & Efficiency

IGNITION

Tools & techniques
to create an ember

LAY

Architecture
to optimize heat

EFFICIENCY

Science of
combustion,
heat not smoke

Introduction: The Keeper of the Clean Flame

The ability to create and control fire is what defined us as a species. Long before we split the atom or built the internet, fire was the first technology: the source of warmth, protection, and cooked food that allowed our ancestors to survive and thrive. To build a fire is not simply a survival skill; it is an act of reconnection—to our history, to the wild world, and to a fundamental process of science.

This book is your guide to mastering firecraft with intention and efficiency. We'll move beyond the simple match strike and flimsy campfire to explore sustainable methods, natural tinders, and advanced fire structures used by cultures throughout history and optimized by modern science. Our goal is to make you a Keeper of the Clean Flame—someone who can reliably create fire, manage its energy, and leave no trace of its passing.

We will focus on the three pillars of modern firecraft:

1. **Ignition:** The tools and techniques, from a ferro rod to the ancient bow drill, required to transition energy into an ember.

2. **Lay:** The architecture of the fire structure itself—how you arrange fuel to optimize heat for cooking, warmth, or signaling.

3. **Efficiency:** The science of combustion, ensuring you extract the maximum energy from the minimum amount of fuel, creating heat, not smoke.

Mastering these pillars is the foundation of resilience and true environmental stewardship.

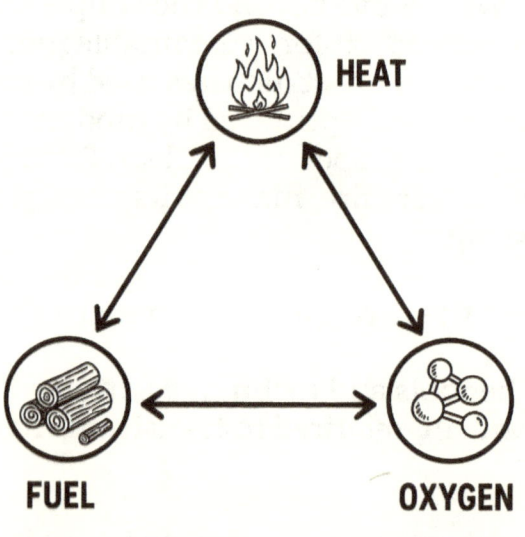

THE FIRE TRIANGLE

Three Elements of Combustion

HEAT

FUEL

OXYGEN

The Fire Triangle Explained

Before you strike a spark, you must understand what fire is: a chemical reaction requiring three components that form a **Fire Triangle.** Remove any one element, and the fire dies.

1. **Fuel:** The material that burns (wood, gas, fabric). To sustain a fire, the fuel must be heated until it releases flammable gases.

2. **Heat:** The energy needed to raise the fuel to its ignition temperature. This is the initial spark or ember, and the sustained heat of the fire keeps the reaction going.

3. **Oxygen:** The air required to chemically combine with the fuel. Proper airflow (draft) is often the most misunderstood and critical component of successful firecraft.

Controlling these three elements is the core skill of a fire keeper.

Fire Ethics and Leave No Trace (LNT)

A responsible fire keeper operates under the principle of **Leave No Trace (LNT)**. This is not just a polite suggestion; it is a critical safety and ethical guideline.

1. **Plan and Prepare:** Check fire bans and weather forecasts before you go. Carry a shovel and water or a fire extinguisher.

2. **The Container:** Whenever possible, use an existing fire ring. If you must build a new fire, use a Mound Fire or Pan Fire to protect the ground from scarring. Never build a fire next to overhanging branches or on top of tree roots.

3. **Source Responsibly:** Only gather wood that is dead and down. Never cut live wood. The best wood snaps cleanly rather than bending.

4. **Extinguish Completely:** This is the most vital safety step. Drown the fire with water, stir the embers until they are cool to the touch, and repeat until absolutely cold. If you cannot touch the remains with your bare hands, the fire is not out. **"Drown, Stir, Drown."**

The Anatomy of Fuel: Tinder, Kindling, and Fuelwood Assessment

Building a fire is like building a house: you start with the foundation (tinder) and gradually add larger support materials (fuelwood).

Stage	Size & Definition	Purpose	Assessment
Tinder	Fine, fibrous material that catches a spark or ember (e.g., cotton, finely shredded bark).	Converts the smallest spark into a sustained flame.	Must be **bone dry.**
Kindling	Pencil-to-thumb thick sticks.	Bridges the gap between the small tinder flame and larger fuel.	Must be dry and should snap crisply when bent.
Fuelwood	Wrist-to-arm thick logs.	Sustains the fire for cooking and warmth.	Hardwoods (oak, hickory) burn long; softwoods (pine, cedar) burn fast and hot.

Cultural Fire: The History of Fire as Medicine and Land Management

The history of fire is inseparable from human culture. For millennia, many Indigenous peoples, particularly in the Americas and Australia, practiced cultural burning (also known as prescribed fire). This wasn't about simply keeping warm; it was a sophisticated tool for shaping the landscape. These intentional, low-intensity burns managed forest health, promoted specific food crops, reduced fuel loads to prevent catastrophic wildfires, and acted as a form of medicine for the land. Our goal of efficiency and clean flame is a direct continuation of this respect for fire as a powerful tool for stewardship.

The foundation of every reliable fire isn't the spark, it's the fuel. Gathering and preparing your tinder, kindling, and fuelwood is where you spend 90% of your time. If you do this job well, ignition will be easy; if you rush it, no tool can save you.

Tinder Type	Source	Key Characteristic
Shredded Bark	Inner bark of Cedar, Juniper, or Birch.	Fluffy, catches a spark quickly. **Birch bark** is especially valuable as it contains oils that make it burn even when wet.
Fungi	**Amadou** (tinder fungus) and **Artist's Conk**.	Catches a spark and holds an ember for a long time, historically used as pocket tinder.
Plant Fluff	**Cattail** or **Milkweed** down.	Extremely fine, ignites easily from a tiny ember, but burns very fast.
Punk Wood/Fatwood	Rotting wood, or pine knots saturated with resin.	**Punk wood** is soft and absorbs heat well; **Fatwood** is highly flammable due to its resin content.

Char Cloth is a perfect prepared tinder. It's cotton or linen fabric heated in a sealed tin, which leaves behind pure carbon. It won't flame, but it catches and holds a spark instantly, allowing you time to place it into your nest.

Feather Sticks and Processing Wet Wood

Finding dry wood in the rain or snow is one of firecraft's greatest challenges. The solution is often inside the wood itself.

Feather sticks are fine shavings of wood left attached to a larger piece. By using a sharp knife to peel thin curls from a piece of dry wood, you expose the dry core material. These curls—the thinner the better—act as kindling that ignites easily.

When dealing with wet logs, the process is called batoning. Use your knife and a heavy stick (the "baton") to strike the spine of the knife, splitting the wet outer shell to access the dry interior wood. This is a tool-intensive method that requires safety and precision.

FEATHER STICKS & PROCESSING WET WOOD

1. FEATHER STICKS: DRY KINDKILING

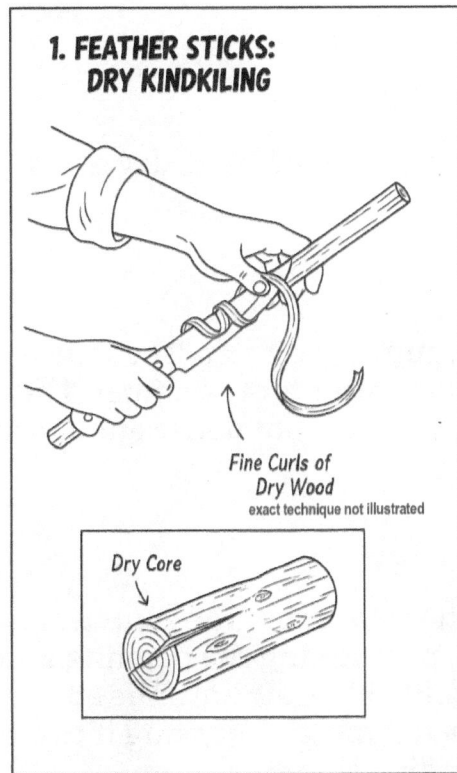

Fine Curls of Dry Wood
exact technique not illustrated

Dry Core

2. BATONING: ACCESSING THE DRY CORE

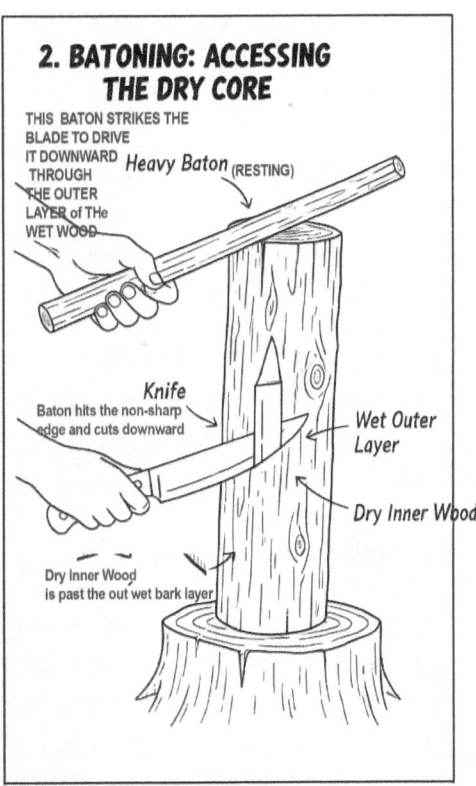

THIS BATON STRIKES THE BLADE TO DRIVE IT DOWNWARD THROUGH THE OUTER LAYER of THE WET WOOD

Heavy Baton (RESTING)

Knife
Baton hits the non-sharp edge and cuts downward

Wet Outer Layer

Dry Inner Wood

Dry Inner Wood is past the out wet bark layer

ADAPTING TO DAMP & CHALLENGING ENVIRONMENTS

The Tinder Nest: Construction and Airflow

A tinder nest is the cradle for your nascent fire. It must be built to protect the fragile coal while allowing maximum airflow to grow it into a flame.

Preparation:

Gather your finest, driest tinder (shredded bark, dry grass, char cloth).

Shape:

Form the material into a loose, cup-like bird's nest shape, leaving a small depression in the center for the ember. The nest should be loose enough to breathe, but dense enough to hold heat.

Transfer and Blow:

Place your glowing ember or char cloth into the center. Hold the nest in your cupped hands, positioning the opening away from the wind. Gently and steadily blow air onto the ember. Do not blast it! The goal is to feed it oxygen, causing it to glow brighter and ignite the surrounding tinder.

IGNITE THE TINDER NEST

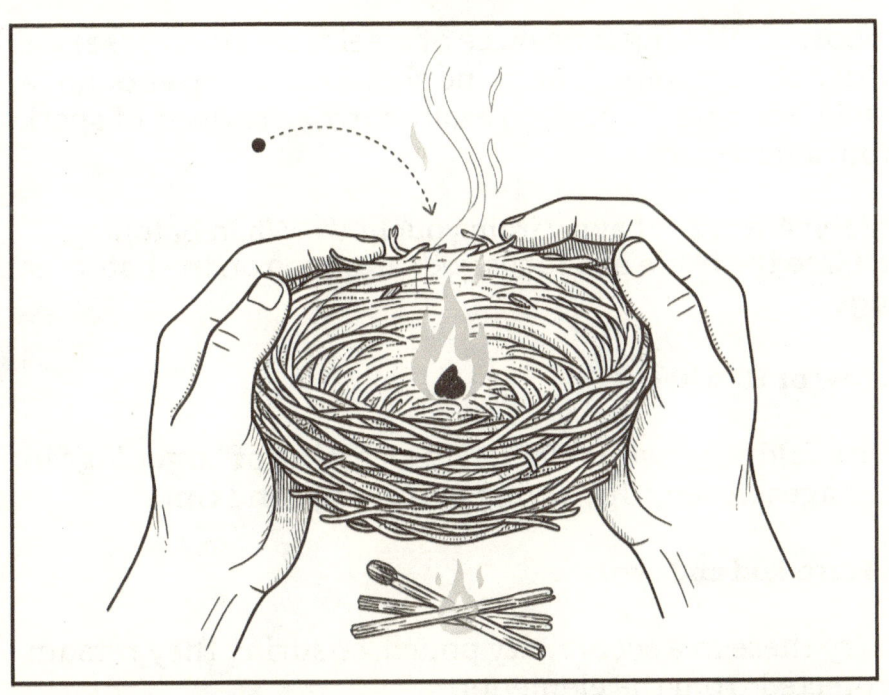

THE CRUCIAL FIRST FLAME

Tool Kit: Knives, Saws, and Safety

Your fire kit is incomplete without proper tools. A well-maintained knife is the single most important tool for fire preparation.

1. Fixed-Blade Knife:

Choose a full-tang (one piece of steel from tip to base) knife with a robust spine. The spine should be sharp enough (a 90-degree angle is best) to easily throw a shower of sparks from a ferro rod.

Safety: Always cut away from your body. When batoning, stabilize the blade and focus your attention on the baton, not the edge.

2. Saw or Hatchet:

Use a folding saw for efficient processing of larger logs into manageable lengths, saving you energy and time.

3. Ferro Rod and Striker.

Carry these in a secure, dry pouch, ensuring they remain protected from the elements.

Remember: You are in charge of your tools. Respect their edges, and always store them safely.

TOOL KIT: KNIVES, SAWS, & SAFETY

Essential Gear for the Fire Keeper.

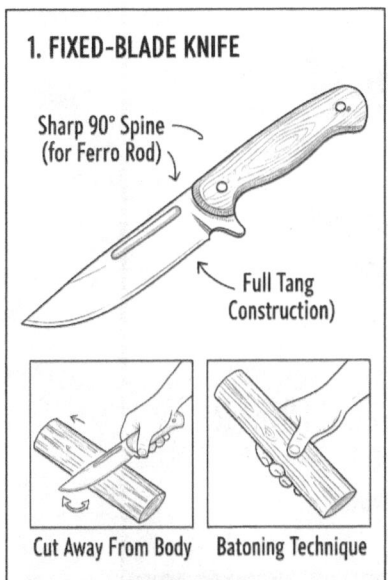

1. FIXED-BLADE KNIFE

Sharp 90° Spine
(for Ferro Rod)

Full Tang
Construction)

Cut Away From Body   Batoning Technique

2. SAW & HATCHET

Folding
Saw

Camp Hatchet

Process Firewiod

3. FERRO ROD & STRIKER

Secure Dry Pouch

RESPECT YOUR TOOLS & PRACTICE SAFETY.

FIRE STARTING: FERRO ROD

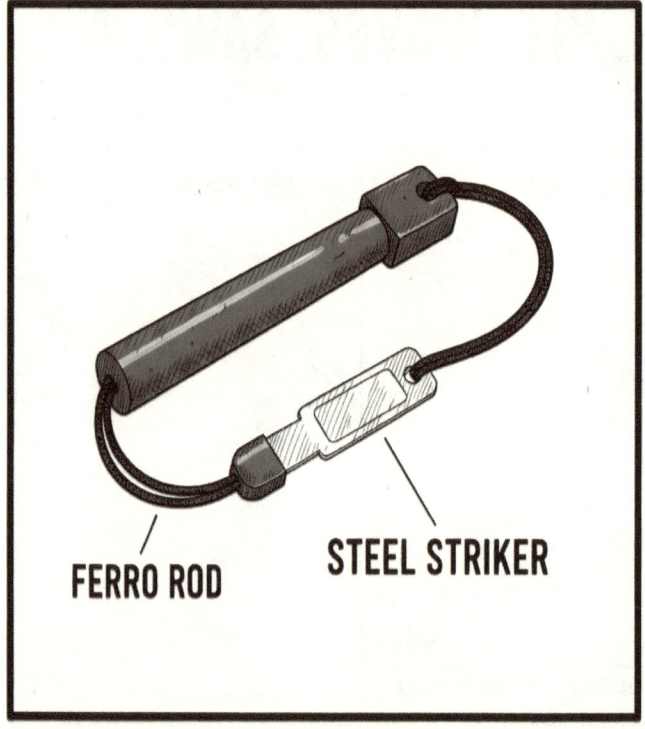

FERRO ROD

STEEL STRIKER

MODERN, RELIABLE SPARKS

While primitive fire is romantic, reliability is paramount. The methods in this chapter are your first line of defense, leveraging modern science and metallurgy.

Ferrocerium Rods: Technique and Reliable Sparking:
The ferrocerium rod (often mistakenly called a "fire steel") is the king of modern survival ignition. This synthetic metal alloy throws incredibly hot - from 3,000∘F to 5,500∘F (1,650∘ C to 3,000∘C), long-lasting sparks that can ignite even slightly damp tinder.

The key to success isn't brute strength, but technique:

Preparation:
Scrape a small pile of ferrocerium dust onto your tinder nest.

Grip:
Place the tip of the rod deep into the tinder nest. Stabilize the rod, keeping it completely still.

Strike:
Use the striker (or the spine of your knife) to pull backwards—away from the tinder—with a swift, hard stroke. By keeping the rod still and moving the striker, you ensure the spark lands exactly where you want it. While some beginners might naturally try to push the striker down the rod into the tinder, the "pull backwards" method is generally superior for consistent and precise ignition. This is because keeping the rod stationary directs all the powerful, hot sparks precisely onto the tinder, rather than scattering them by moving the ignition source itself.

Flint and Steel (Traditional and Modern)

The method that carried civilization through millennia, flint and steel, operates on the principle of percussion.

Traditional:

A high-carbon steel striker is forcefully struck against the sharp edge of a flint or quartz rock. This action shaves off tiny, hot particles of steel, which then ignite char cloth or a specially prepared fungal tinder. The resulting ember must then be carefully transferred to the tinder nest.

Modern:

This method is often confused with the ferro rod. Remember, the ferro rod is the spark-generating material; in traditional flint and steel, the steel is the sacrificial material.

FIRE STARTING: FLINT & STEEL

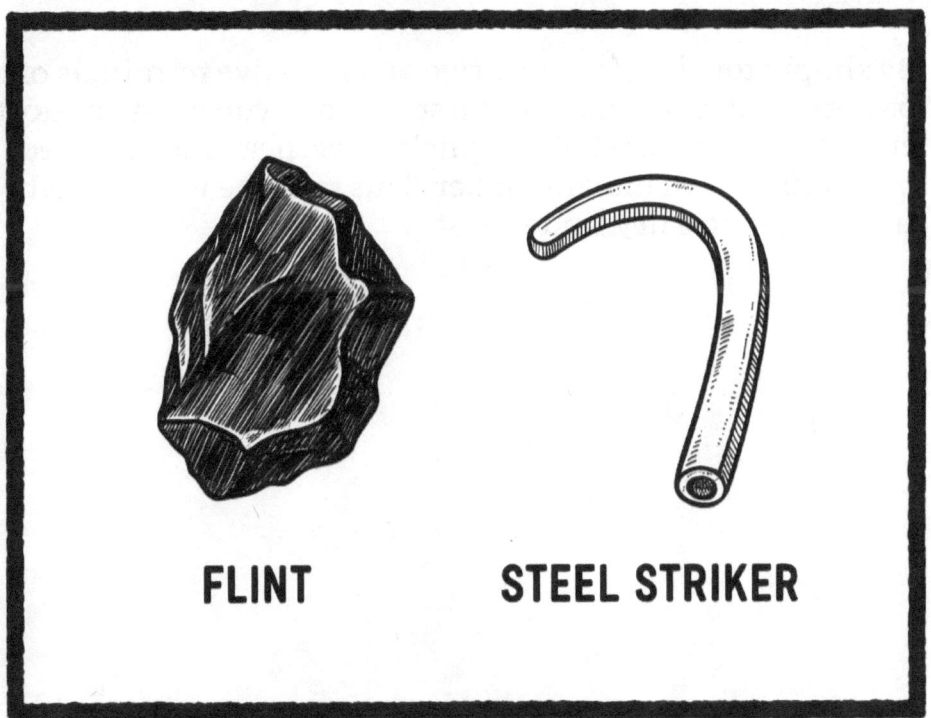

FLINT   STEEL STRIKER

ANCIENT METHOD, RELIABLE SPARK

The Electrical Shortcut: Batteries and Steel Wool

This is an emergency technique, but highly effective. It requires a 9-volt battery and fine-grade steel wool (#0000 is best).

By simply touching the positive and negative terminals of the battery simultaneously to the steel wool, you create a short circuit. The fine steel fibers quickly overheat and glow red hot, acting as an instant ember. This must be immediately transferred to a dry tinder nest.

THE ELECTRICAL SHORTCUT:
INSTANT IGNITION

1. THE SETUP

2. THE SPARK & EMBER

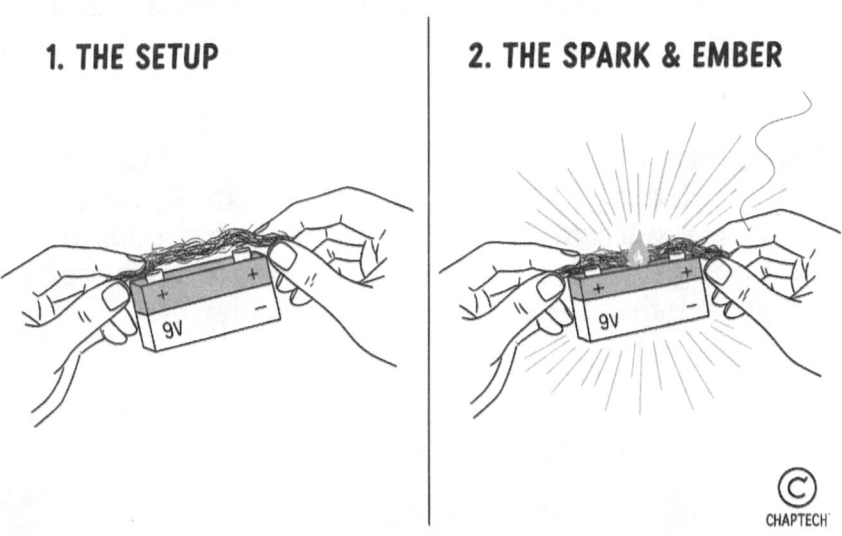

INSTANT FIRE FROM EVERYDAY ITEMS

Solar and Optical Fire

Any curved, transparent, or reflective surface can focus the sun's energy into a point of intense heat. This method works perfectly on a sunny day but is useless under cloud cover.

The Lens: The classic method uses a magnifying glass. Eyeglasses (reading glasses especially), binoculars, and even the curved base of a thick piece of ice (polished by hand) can work as a lens to focus sunlight directly onto black or charred tinder.

The Reflector: You can create a concave (curved inward) mirror by polishing the bottom of a soda can. By smearing the aluminum with toothpaste, dirt, or even chocolate, and then polishing it with a soft cloth, you create a mirror finish capable of focusing the sun's rays onto tinder.

Solar and Optical Fire:

FREE FIRE FROM THE SUN'S RAYS

1. THE LENS:
MAGNIFYING GLASS

2. THE REFLECTOR:
COKE CAN BOTTOM

Magnifying Lens

HOLD STEADY + FOCUS

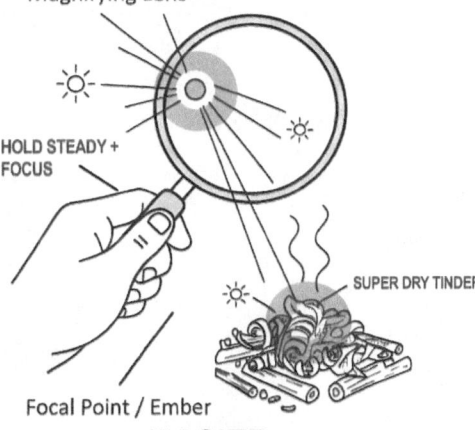
SUPER DRY TINDER

Polished Reflector (Concave Mirror)

Focal Point / Ember

Reflected Focus

Heat

EASIER

MORE DIFFICULT

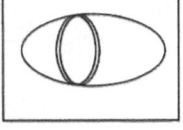

FOR EACH TECHNIQUE PRACTICE WILL MAKE IT EASIER

CHAPTECH
APPLIED VERNACLUAR

HARNESSING THE SUN ENERGY FOR INSTANT IGNITION

BOW DRILL FIRE STARTER

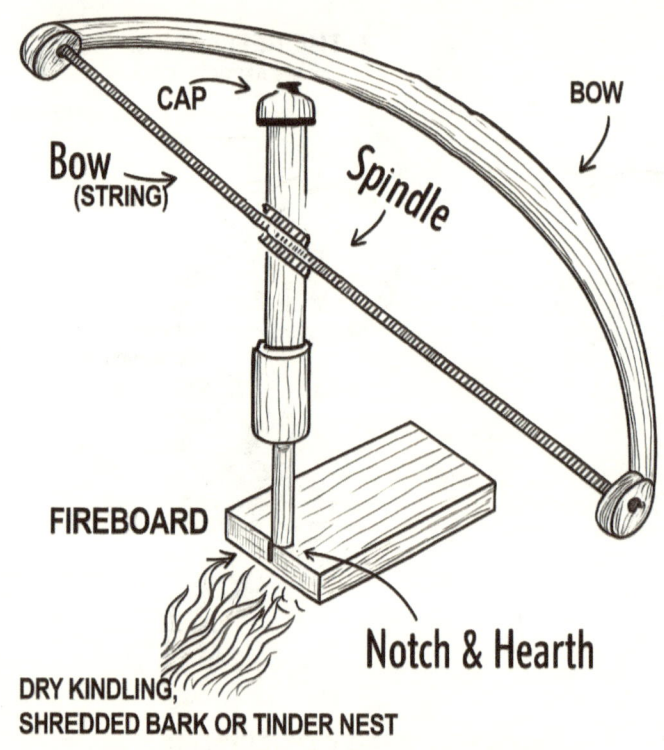

CAP

BOW

Bow
(STRING)

Spindle

FIREBOARD

Notch & Hearth

DRY KINDLING,
SHREDDED BARK OR TINDER NEST

Friction fire is the ultimate test of skill, patience, and knowledge of wood selection. These methods rely on rubbing wood against wood to create heat, converting the dust byproduct into a glowing coal through rapid, concentrated friction.

The Bow Drill: The Most Reliable Friction System

The bow drill is the most common and arguably the easiest friction method to master because it allows you to sustain speed and apply consistent downward pressure simultaneously.

The system requires four components:

Fireboard (Hearth): A soft, dry piece of wood (e.g., cedar, cottonwood).

Spindle (Drill): A slightly harder, straight stick that spins in a divot on the fireboard.

Bow: A flexible stick with a cord that loops around the spindle.

Handhold (Socket): A piece of hard wood or stone used to apply downward pressure to the top of the spindle.

The key is to saw the bow back and forth, spinning the spindle rapidly in a small hole cut near a V-notch in the fireboard.

Wood dust collects in the notch and, when the temperature hits 800° F (427°C), it ignites into a hot coal.

The Hand Drill: Technique and Two-Man Variations

The Hand Drill is simpler in construction but far more difficult to execute. It requires no cordage or bow.

You spin a long, straight spindle between your palms, while applying downward pressure into the fireboard. The difficulty lies in maintaining pressure while repositioning your hands as they slide down the spindle. It is typically effective only in dry climates.

The Two-Man Variation mitigates the difficulty by having one person stabilize and press down on the spindle, while the second person uses a cord or thong wrapped around the spindle to generate the spinning motion.

THE HAND DRILL:
SIMPLE FRICTION FIRE

1. THE SET-UP & SPIN

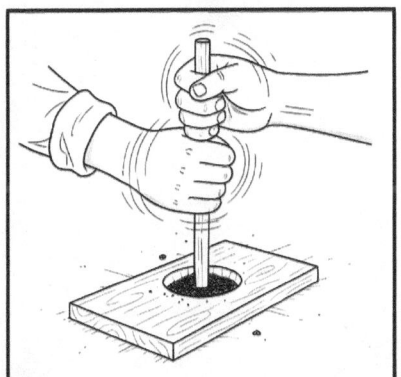

2. THE EMBER

Tinder Nest

ANCIENT FIRE FROM WOOD & EFFORT

CHAPTECH

The Fire Plough: Plowing for Coal in Simpler Wood

The Fire Plough is another classic friction method, historically used in regions like Polynesia.

You take a pointed stick (the plough) and vigorously rub it back and forth down a straight groove cut into a fireboard. This "plowing" action pushes the heated wood dust forward into a small pile at the end of the groove. With enough speed and pressure, this pile will ignite into a coal.

THE FIRE PLOUGH:
SIMPLE FURROW OF FLAME

THE EMBER

ANCIENT FIRE FROM
WOOD & EFFORT

The Fire Saw and Fire Thong: Sawing Friction

These methods are common in the tropics, where soft, fibrous bamboo is often the material of choice.

Fire Saw: A piece of wood or bamboo is sawn quickly across the edge of a second piece of wood/bamboo until the friction creates an ember in the dust.

Fire Thong: Similar to the saw, a thin strip of bamboo or cord (the thong) is rapidly pulled back and forth, generating friction on a stationary wooden base.

PRIMITIVE FIRE STARTING: FRICTION METHODS

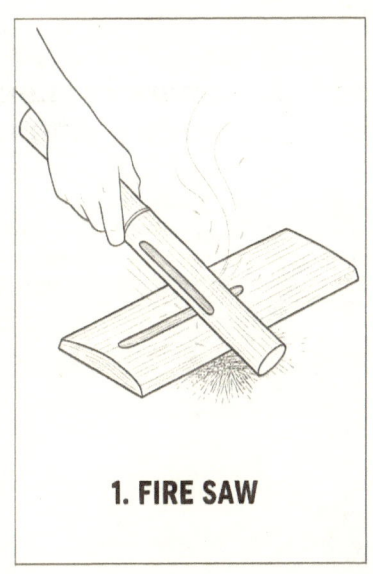

1. FIRE SAW

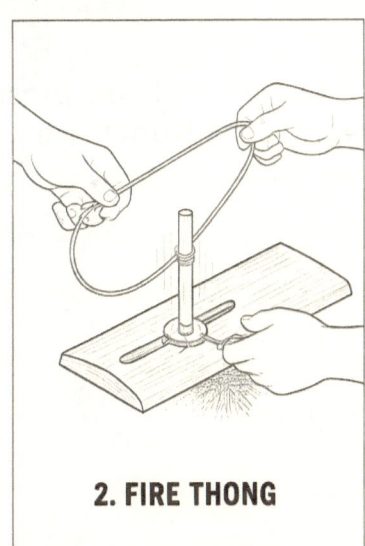

2. FIRE THONG

ANCIENT WISDOM, ESSENTIAL SKILL

Fire by Compression: The Fire Piston: Theory and Operation

The Fire Piston is a unique, niche survival tool based entirely on physics, popular in Southeast Asia.

A small piece of tinder (usually char cloth) is placed into a tightly fitting cylinder. The plunger is then driven down rapidly.

This sudden, violent compression of air generates enough heat to ignite the tinder, which is then quickly withdrawn to the tinder nest.

THE FIRE PISTON:
COMPRESSION IGNITION

1. COMPRESS

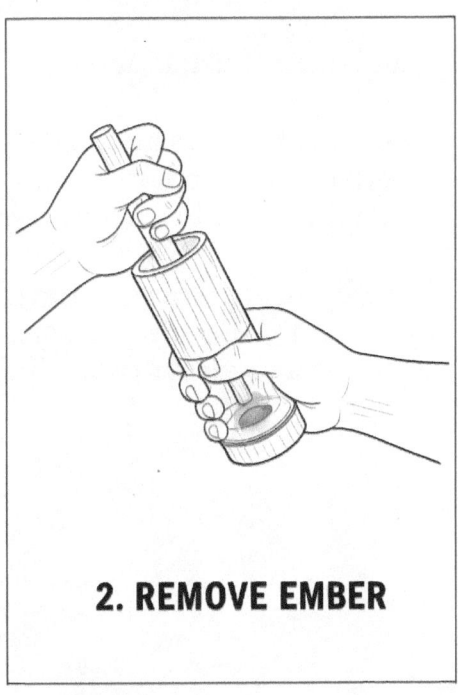

2. REMOVE EMBER

INSTANT FIRE FROM THE PHYSICS OF AIR

The Pump Drill: Mechanical Advantage in Friction

The pump drill is an ingenious variation of the spindle and fireboard method, using a weighted flywheel and a crossbar to drive the spindle up and down with great speed and efficiency.

Used by some North American Indigenous groups, it requires two hands, allowing the user to maintain a consistent rhythm with far less effort than the hand drill.

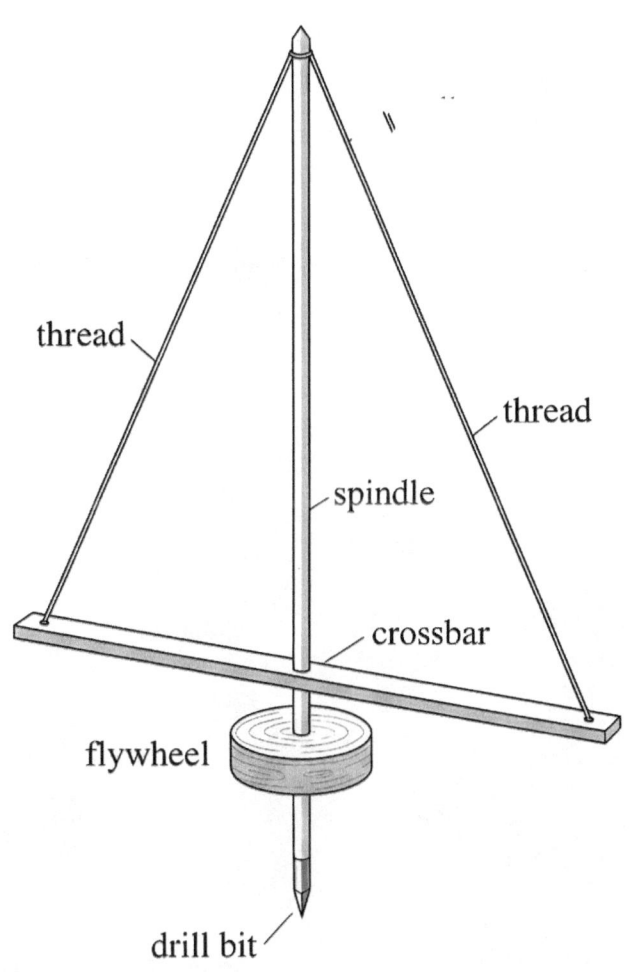

thread

thread

spindle

crossbar

flywheel

drill bit

Part III: The Architecture of Fire
Chapter 5: Classic and Elemental Fire Lays

The fire lay is the physical structure of your fire—its architecture. The way you stack your fuel dictates how quickly it ignites, how much heat it produces, and whether that heat is optimized for cooking or staying warm. Start small, build slowly, and always leave space for air to circulate.

The Teepee and the Lean-To: Fast Heat and Wind Management

These are the simplest and most common lays, ideal for getting a quick, bright fire going.

The Teepee: The classic, fast-ignition lay. Place your tinder nest in the center, surround it with fine kindling, and lean progressively larger pieces of fuel against the center in a cone shape. Leave a gap on the downwind side for ignition and airflow. This lay naturally directs smoke upwards and creates strong vertical draft, leading to tall, fast flames.

The Lean-To: Excellent for fighting wind and dampness. Find a large log or rock to serve as a windbreak and structural support. Lean your kindling and tinder against this support at an angle. The support protects the flame from wind while radiating heat back into the fire.

The Teepee: Fast Ignition Lay

- Fuel Wood Kindkling
- Airflow / Downwind Ignition Gap
- Strong Vertical Draft
- Tinder Nest

The Lean-To: Wind Management Lay

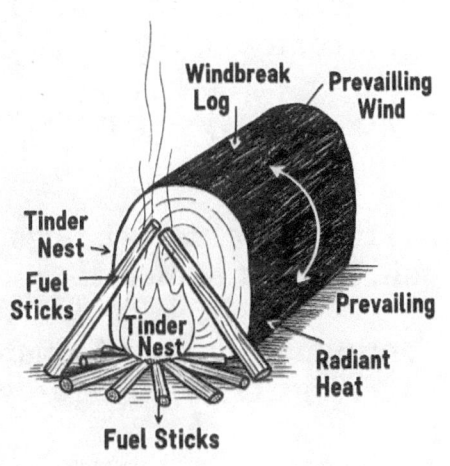

- Windbreak Log
- Prevailling Wind
- Tinder Nest
- Fuel Sticks
- Tinder Nest
- Prevailing Radiant Heat
- Fuel Sticks

Simple Lays for Quick, Bright Fires

The Log Cabin: The Classic, Stable Cooking Fire

The **Log Cabin** is the most stable and predictable lay, making it an exceptional choice for **cooking**.

1. Start with your tinder and kindling (a Teepee works well) in the center.

2. Lay two small logs parallel on opposite sides of the kindling base.

3. Lay two slightly longer logs perpendicular across the first pair, creating a square.

4. Continue building the square structure with progressively larger logs, creating a sturdy box around the initial fire.

5. As the center fire burns, the logs of the cabin walls are pre-heated, allowing the fire to burn slowly and evenly. The flat top of the structure provides a natural, stable rest for pots, pans, or grills.

Building the
Log Cabin

The Stable
Cooking Fire

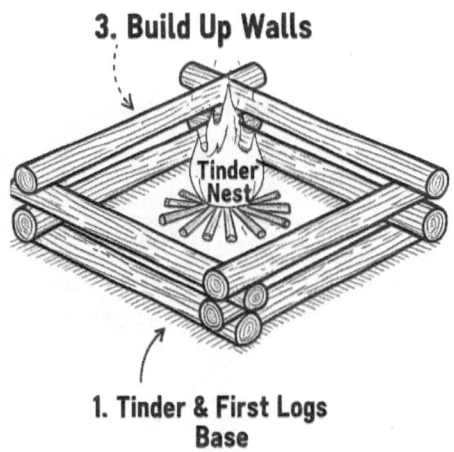

3. Build Up Walls

Tinder Nest

1. Tinder & First Logs
Base

Pre-heated
Logs

Flat, Stable
Cooking Surfac

Slow, Even
Burn

The Log Cabin: Clasic, Cooking Fire

The Criss-Cross (Upside-Down) Lay: Low-Maintenance and Long Burn

Also known as the **Top-Down fire**, this method is counter-intuitive but incredibly efficient, making it excellent for staying warm over a long night.

1. Lay down 3–4 of your largest fuel logs parallel on the bottom.

2. Stack succeeding layers perpendicularly, using smaller and smaller wood, like a pyramid.

3. Place your finest kindling and tinder right on the very top.

4. You light the fire on the top layer.

The flame burns slowly downward, igniting the layers beneath it only when they've been fully pre-heated by the layer above. This creates a sustained, low-smoke fire that requires minimal attention for hours.

The Criss-Cross Lay: Low-Maintenance Fire

1. Tinder on Top

2. Largest Fuel Logs on Bottom

The Upside-Down: Long, Slow Burn

Flame Burns Down

Pre-heated Layers

Sustained Heat

Long Burn, Low Smoke Fire

The Star Fire (Indian Fire Lay): Fuel Conservation and Controlled Feeding

The Star Fire is the most economical fire lay, designed to conserve large fuel logs while maintaining a small, hot center.

1. Arrange 4–6 large logs like the spokes of a wheel, with their ends meeting at a central tinder fire.

2. As the ends burn down, you simply push the logs inward toward the center of the fire with your foot or a stick.

This method allows you to control the size and fuel consumption precisely and is ideal when firewood is scarce.

THE STAR FIRE (INDIAN FIRE LAY): FUEL CONSERVATION
CONTROLLED FEEDING

1. INITIAL LAY & BURN

2. CONTROLLED FEEDING

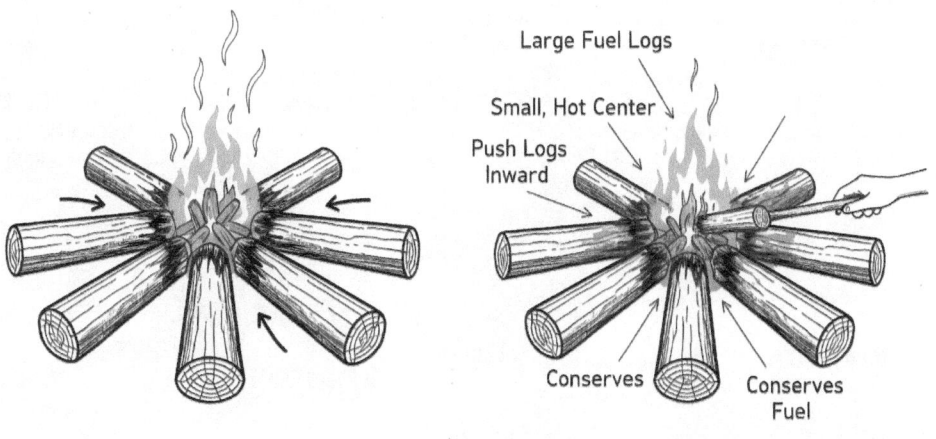

Large Fuel Logs

Small, Hot Center

Push Logs Inward

Conserves

Conserves Fuel

ECONOMICAL FIRE FOR SCARCE FUEL

1. CONSTRUCTION & AIRFLOW

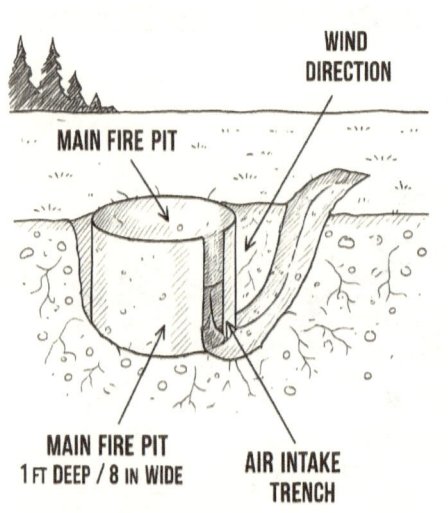

WIND DIRECTION

MAIN FIRE PIT

MAIN FIRE PIT
1 FT DEEP / 8 IN WIDE

AIR INTAKE TRENCH

2. STEALTH & HIGH HEAT

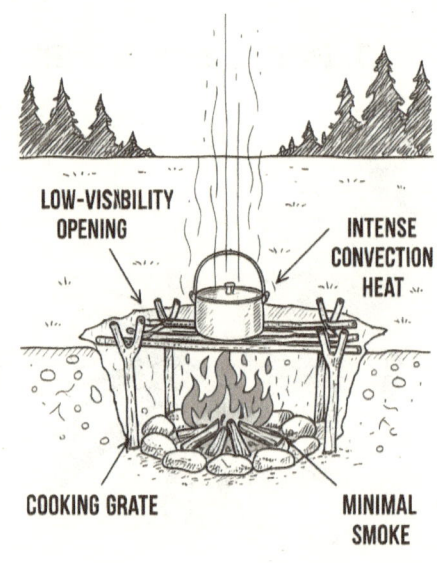

LOW-VISXBILITY OPENING

INTENSE CONVECTION HEAT

COOKING GRATE

MINIMAL SMOKE

THE DAKOTA FIRE PIT: STEALTH, EFFICIENCY, & CONTROLED COOKING.

When your environment demands adaptation—whether for stealth, efficiency, or working on challenging terrain—you need specialized structures.

The Dakota Fire Pit: Stealth, Airflow, and Convection

The **Dakota Fire Pit** is a highly efficient, low-visibility fire that uses advanced airflow principles.

1. **Dig Two Pits:** Dig a small, cylindrical fire pit (approx. 1 foot deep, 8 inches wide).

2. **Dig the Air Intake:** Dig a separate air trench leading from the surface down to the bottom of the main pit. This trench acts like a bellows or chimney, drawing a massive amount of oxygen directly to the base of the fire.

The result is a nearly smokeless, extremely hot fire that is shielded from the wind and nearly invisible from a distance. The intense heat makes it superb for cooking, though it requires effort to build.

The Keyhole Fire Pit: Zone Cooking and Ember Control

If your priority is gourmet camp cooking, the **Keyhole Fire Pit** is your best friend.

1. Construct a standard circle or square fire pit, then attach a narrow, elongated extension, creating a shape that looks like a keyhole. You build a large, hot fire in the main circle.

2. When you need to cook, you drag the hot, perfectly formed **embers** into the narrow extension (the "keyhole").

This allows you to regulate the temperature of the cooking zone precisely, without the inconsistent heat of active flame.

THE KEYHOLE FIRE PIT: ZONE COOKING

1. BUILD & BURN

2. COOKING WITH EMBERS

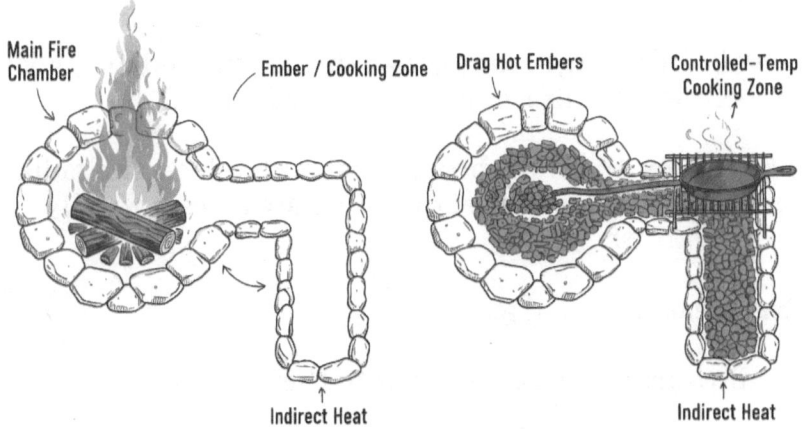

Main Fire Chamber

Ember / Cooking Zone

Indirect Heat

Drag Hot Embers

Controlled-Temp Cooking Zone

Indirect Heat

PERFECT HEAT FOR GOURMET CAMP COOKING

The Reflector Wall and Trench Fire: Maximizing Radiant Heat

The most effective method for staying warm in a fixed camp is using a reflector.

Reflector Wall:

1. Build a wall (from large stones, logs, or even packed dirt) about 2–3 feet behind your fire, angling slightly forward.

2. As the fire burns, the wall absorbs heat and reflects the radiant heat back toward your shelter or sitting area, dramatically increasing warmth.

Trench Fire: Ideal on sloped ground.

1. Dig a shallow trench perpendicular to the wind.

2. Build your fire in the trench, which acts as a wind tunnel, pulling air along its length and creating a strong, focused heat line.

MAXIMIZING RADIANT HEAT
THE REFLECTOR WALL & TRENCH FIRE

1. THE REFLECTOR WALL:
DIRECTED WARMTH

Radiant Heat
Directed
to Shelter

2. THE TRENCH FIRE:
FOCUSED HEAT LINE

Trench Dug
into Slope

Prevailing
Wind

Strong Airflow

Focused
Heat Line

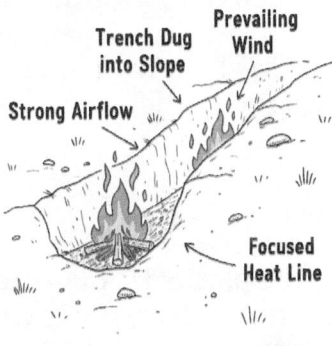

STAYING WARM & EFFICIENT IN FIXED CAMPS

The Platform and Raft Fire: Building a Base in Snow or Wet Ground

In environments with deep snow, wet marshy ground, or solid rock, you cannot build directly on the surface.

The Platform:

Lay down a bed of large, thick, green logs, stones, or thick packed dirt. This platform acts as an insulation layer, keeping the fire dry and preventing heat from melting through the snow or transferring into the ground (which would quench the fire). The heat is directed upward.

The Raft:

Similar to the platform, but often used to build a temporary fire on large boulders or rocky areas where a direct fire would permanently scar the surface.

THE PLATFORM AND RAFT FIRE:
BUILDING A BASE IN SNOW OR WET GROUND

1. THE PLATFORM:
FOR SNOW & WET GROUND

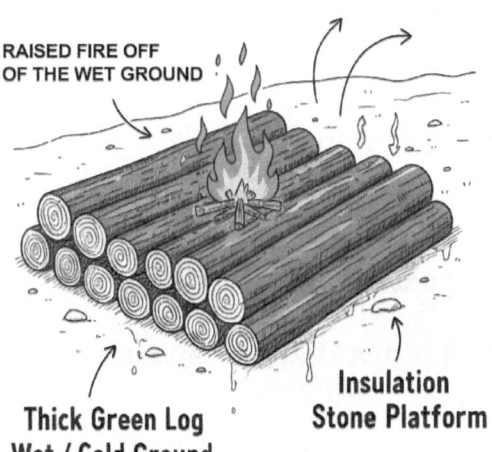

RAISED FIRE OFF
OF THE WET GROUND

Thick Green Log
Wet / Cold Ground

Insulation
Stone Platform

2. THE RAFT FIRE:
FOR ROCKY SURFACES

FIRE BURING ON A ROCK

Stone (Found or Moved)

No-Trace Fire
on Solid Rock

STAYING WARM & COOKING IN CHALLENIGT TERRAIN

The Stone Boil and Mound Fire: Advanced Leave No Trace Cooking

These methods offer primitive cooking and minimal impact.

The Stone Boil: An ancient technique for heating water or stew without metal pots.

1. You build a fire with stones nearby.

2. Once the stones are searingly hot, you use tongs or two sticks to drop them directly into a container of water (a bark vessel, a bladder, or a wooden bowl).

The heat instantly transfers, bringing the water to a boil.

Mound Fire: The gold standard for LNT fire.

1. You clear a large area and then lay down a tarp or plastic sheet.

2. Cover the sheet with 4–6 inches of mineral soil or sand, creating a raised platform.

3. Build your fire on top of the mound.

When finished, you douse the fire, retrieve the stones, and then dump the mound contents back into the surrounding area, leaving the ground underneath untouched.

PRIMITIVE & LEAVE NO TRACE COOKING

1. THE STONE BOIL: ANCIENT WATER HEATING

2. THE MOUND FIRE: L.N.T. COOKING PLATFORM

Hot Stones in Fire

Bark/Wood Vessel

Boiling Water

Tong-Sticks

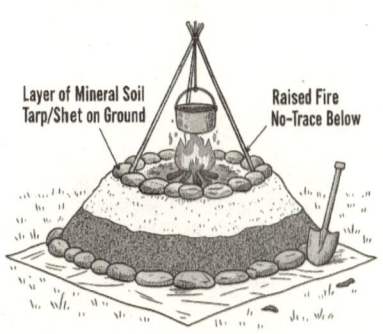

Layer of Mineral Soil Tarp/Shet on Ground

Raised Fire No-Trace Below

ADVANCED METHODS FOR MINIMAL IMPACT & PRIMITIVE COOKING

Chapter 7: High-Efficiency Stoves and Containers

Moving beyond open fire lays, high-efficiency stoves and contained burns represent the ultimate commitment to sustainability and minimal impact. These systems manipulate the combustion triangle to ensure almost complete burning of fuel, producing maximum heat with minimal smoke and soot.

The Rocket Stove: Principles of Chimney Draft and Insulation

The Rocket Stove is one of the fastest and most efficient cooking tools you can build. It achieves nearly perfect combustion by focusing on three principles:

Insulation: The burning chamber is insulated (usually by clay, earth, or a double-walled metal jacket) to keep the heat focused on the fuel, accelerating the release of flammable gases.

Chimney Draft: The unique L- or J-shaped chamber creates a strong vertical draft, pulling massive amounts of oxygen into the burn chamber and forcing hot exhaust gases up a chimney.

Horizontal Feed: Fuel (usually small sticks and kindling) is fed horizontally into the hot burn tunnel, where it vaporizes quickly.

The result is a roaring, jet-like flame that is excellent for fast cooking and boiling water, requiring only a fraction of the wood an open fire would consume.

The Rocket Stove

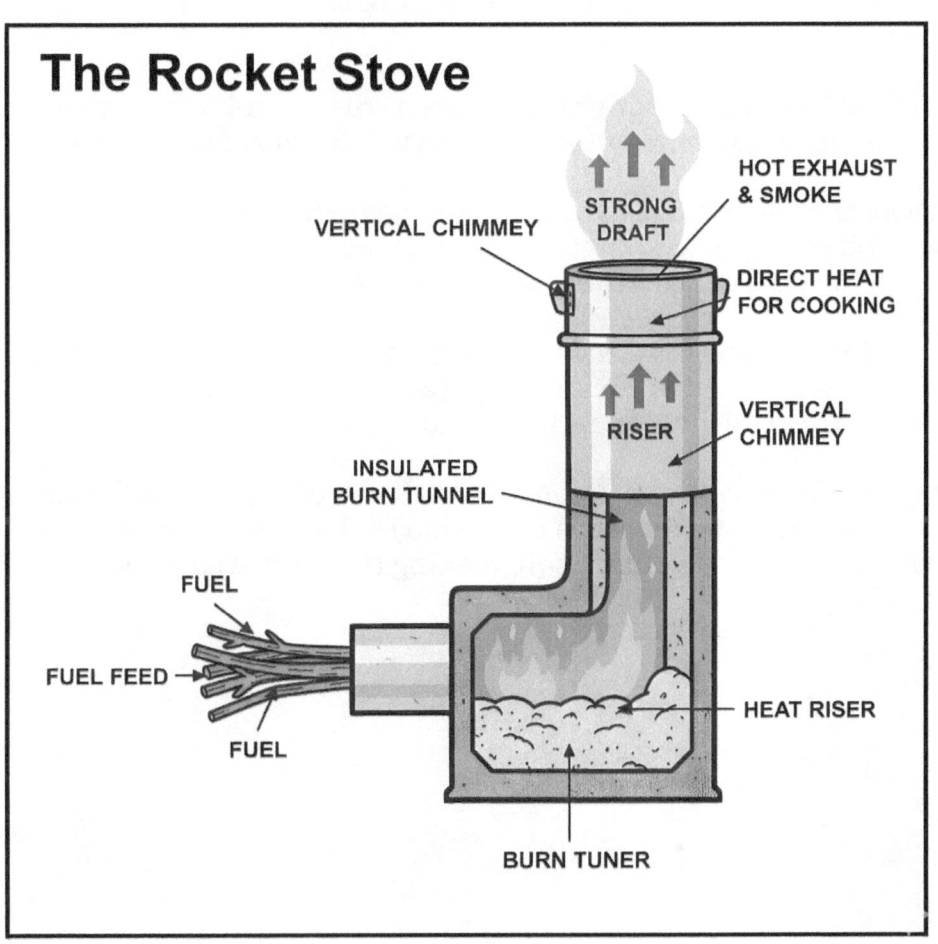

VERTICAL CHIMMEY

STRONG DRAFT

HOT EXHAUST & SMOKE

DIRECT HEAT FOR COOKING

RISER

VERTICAL CHIMMEY

INSULATED BURN TUNNEL

FUEL

FUEL FEED

FUEL

HEAT RISER

BURN TUNER

TLUD (Top-Lit Updraft Gasifier): Making Biochar and Burning Clean

The TLUD (Top-Lit Updraft) gasifier is a true clean-burning marvel, producing almost zero smoke and a valuable byproduct: **biochar**.

Mechanism: The stove uses a primary chamber filled with fuel (wood chips or pellets) that is lit only at the top. As the fire burns down, the heat gasifies the lower, unburned wood.

Clean Burn: These flammable gases are then mixed with secondary oxygen and ignited in a high-temperature zone, leading to a "gas reburn" that consumes nearly all smoke particles.

Biochar: Once the fire has consumed all the gases, the remaining solid material is pure charcoal (biochar), which can be quenched, ground, and used to enrich soil, making the system carbon-negative.

TLUD (TOP-LIT UPDRAFT GASIFIER

MAKING BIOCHAR AND BURNING CLEAN

1. MECHANISM & CLEAN COMBUSTION

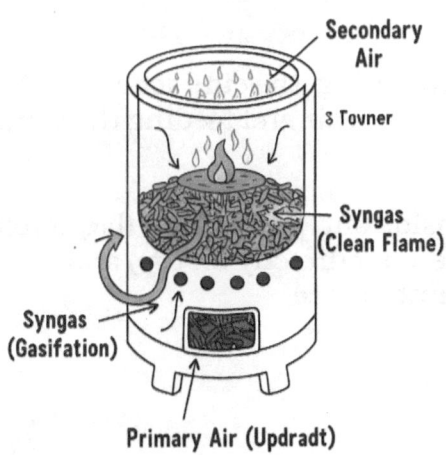

Secondary Air

3 Tovner

Syngas (Clean Flame)

Syngas (Gasifation)

Primary Air (Updradt)

2. THE BIOCHAR BYPRODUCT

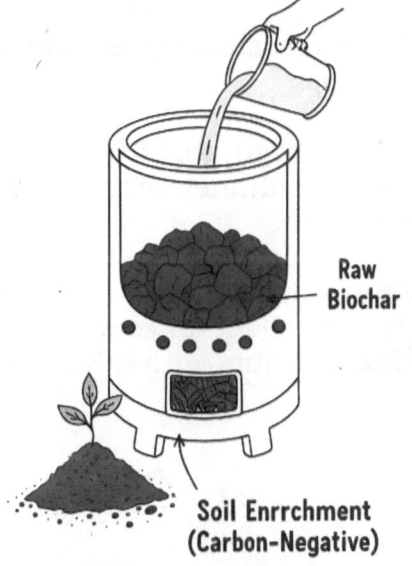

Raw Biochar

Soil Enrrchment (Carbon-Negative)

SMOKELESS FIRE & FERTILE SOIL

The Swedish Torch (Log Candle): A Vertical, Contained Burn

The Swedish Torch (or Log Candle) offers a contained, all-in-one source of heat, light, and a stable cooking platform.

1. Take a thick, dry log and cut it vertically into four or six sections, stopping a few inches short of the bottom. The cuts should form a tight "X" or star pattern.

2. Start a small fire (using tinder and pitch) in the center cuts at the top.

As the fire begins to burn down into the log, the cuts act as miniature chimney channels, drawing in air and feeding the central combustion.

The torch burns slowly from the inside out, providing a flat, stable surface excellent for cooking (place a pot directly on top) and lasting for hours with minimal maintenance.

THE SWEDISH TORCH (LOG CANDLE)
VERTICAL, CONTAINED HEAT & COOKING

1. CONSTRUCTION

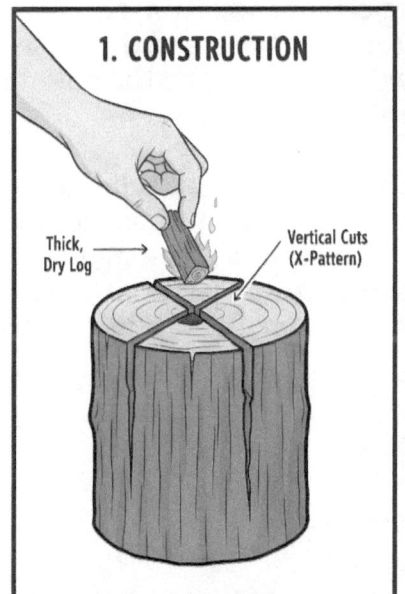

Thick, Dry Log →

Vertical Cuts (X-Pattern)

2. VERTICAL BURN & COOKING

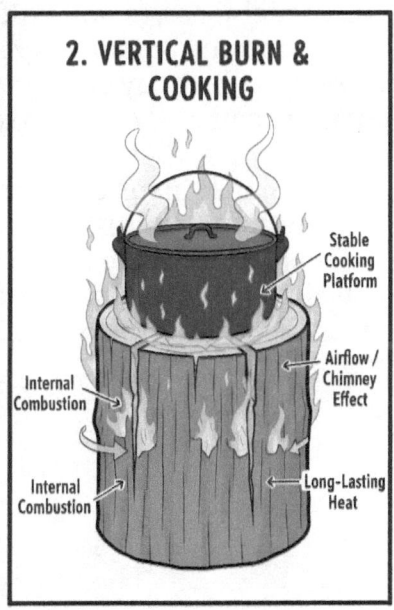

Stable Cooking Platform

Airflow / Chimney Effect

Internal Combustion

Internal Combustion

Long-Lasting Heat

VERTICAL, CONTAINED HEAT & COOKING

Improvised Stoves: Hobo Cans and Konro-Style Grills

Necessity is the mother of invention, and simple improvisation can turn trash into a highly efficient stove.

Hobo Stove (Can Stove): A very fast, temporary cooking stove made from a large metal can (e.g., a coffee can or industrial tin). Holes are punched around the bottom edge for air intake, and the top is cut open to create a chimney effect. Fuel is fed through the opening, and a pot can be placed over the top.

Konro-Style Grills: Inspired by traditional Japanese charcoal grills, this method uses high-quality embers in a small, contained, insulated box (often made from fire bricks or a small metal box). The small size and insulation focus maximum heat onto the cooking surface, making it superior for controlled grilling and searing small items.

Improvised STOVES

HOBO STOVE

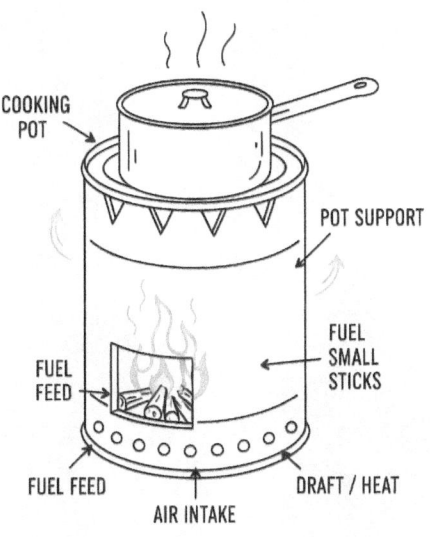

COOKING POT

POT SUPPORT

FUEL FEED

FUEL SMALL STICKS

FUEL FEED

AIR INTAKE

DRAFT / HEAT

KONRO GRILL (BRICK STYLE)

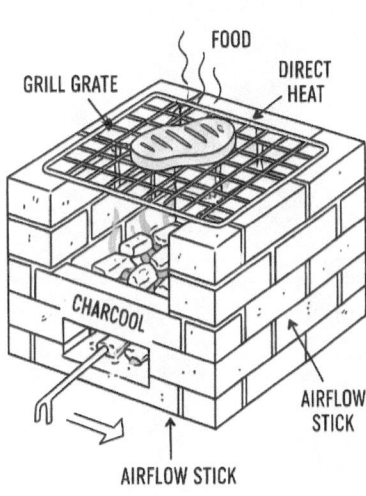

FOOD

GRILL GRATE

DIRECT HEAT

CHARCOOL

AIRFLOW STICK

AIRFLOW STICK

Conclusion: The Mastery of Fire

You have journeyed from the philosophy of fire to its most sophisticated applications. The final step in mastering firecraft is choosing the right tool for the right job. A fire built for cooking is a poor fire for warmth, and a fire built for warmth is too fuel-hungry for survival.

The Fire Utility Matrix: Choosing the Best Lay for Warmth, Cooking, and Signal

Before you strike your first spark, mentally consult this matrix. This final evaluation ensures your effort, fuel, and impact are perfectly aligned with your immediate needs.

Fire Lay / Stove	Primary Use	Fuel Efficiency		Key Advantage
Rocket Stove	Fast Cooking / Boiling	Very High	Low	Extreme speed/minimal smoke.
Reflector Wall	**Staying Warm**	Medium	High	Maximizes radiant heat into shelter.
Criss-Cross	**Overnight Warmth**	High	Low	Burns for hours without tending.
Keyhole Pit	**Gourmet Cooking**	Medium	Low	Precise heat control via embers.
Dakota Pit	Stealth / Fast Cooking	Medium-High	Very Low	Highly concealed and wind-resistant.
Log Cabin	Group Cooking	Medium		Stable platform for pots.

Final Reflections and The Firekeeper's Pledge

The Keeper of the Clean Flame understands that fire is a privilege, not a right. It is a source of power that requires *reverence and respect*.

Practice your skills often, especially the primitive methods, and always be prepared to **Drown, Stir, Drown** until the ashes are cold.

Carry this knowledge forward, and may your fires always be clean, efficient, and well-contained.

TROUBLESHOOTING THE COMBUSTION TRIANGLE

Fixing the Fire Triangle: A Guide to Common Problems

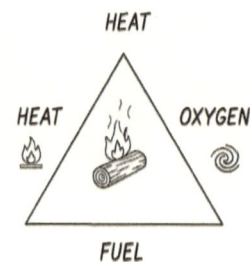

HEAT

HEAT   OXYGEN

FUEL

1. Thick, White Smoke

 Inicmplete Combustion
(fuel too cold)

Solution: ADD AIR (blow tube, gaps in lay) &
(Finer Kindkling)

2. Ember Won't Ignite Tinder

  Small Ember / Damp Tinder

Solution: DRY TINDER (fluff) & INCREASE
HEAT HEAT (Char Cloth / Fatwood)

3. Fire Burns Out Quickly

  Insuificiont Kindkling / Smothering

Solution: BUILD SLOVER (stable flame) &
CLEAR AIRFLOW (lift lay)

Chapter 8: Troubleshooting and Environmental Adaptation

Even the most prepared fire keeper faces challenges. Fire is a reaction governed by the environment; a good craftsperson knows how to recognize a problem and adapt their lay or technique to overcome it.

Troubleshooting the Combustion Triangle

When your fire fails, it's almost always due to an imbalance in the Fire Triangle.

Symptom	Probable Cause	Solution
Thick, White Smoke	Incomplete combustion (fuel too cold).	**Add Air:** Increase the draft using a blow tube or create gaps in the lay. **Add Heat:** Start with finer kindling or switch to dryer wood.
Ember Won't Ignite Tinder	Ember is too small or tinder is too loose/damp.	**Dry Tinder:** Fluff and aerate the tinder nest, removing any damp fibers. **Increase Heat:** Use a small piece of Char Cloth or Fatwood to receive the ember.
Fire Burns Out Quickly	Insufficient kindling or fuel added too quickly.	**Build Slower:** Don't skip the step between kindling and small fuelwood. Wait until the flame is stable before adding larger sticks.
Flames Die Low	Starvation of oxygen (smothering).	**Clear Airflow:** Lift the fire lay slightly (use two larger logs as a base) or clear the side air vents (e.g., in a Dakota Pit).

Fire in the Rain and Snow

Wet environments require two critical adaptations: accessing dry fuel and building an elevated base.

Accessing Dry Wood: Utilize the Batoning technique (Chapter 2) to split open dead, downed logs. The core of a log is often perfectly dry, even if the exterior is saturated. Focus on resinous woods like pine or juniper, which contain natural flammable oils.

Creating a Dry Base: Never build a fire directly on wet earth or snow. Use the Platform Fire method, constructing a base with large, green (non-flammable) logs or flat stones. This keeps the heat separated from the moisture, preventing the fire from quenching itself.

Windbreaks and Shelters: Wind not only cools the flame but drives moisture into the fire. Use a Lean-To structure or natural barriers (boulders, large logs) to protect the ignition zone.

Extreme Cold and Survival Fire

In extreme cold, fire is life, and the goal shifts entirely to maximizing radiant heat for survival.

The Reflector System: The single best survival technique is pairing a low-burning, dense fire (like the Criss-Cross lay) with a large Reflector Wall built directly behind it. Position your shelter opposite the fire so the reflected heat is constantly directed at you.

Heat Sink: Build your fire on a layer of large, flat stones. The stones absorb and store heat, radiating warmth long after the flames have subsided. Ensure any stones you use are completely dry; wet or porous stones can explode when rapidly heated.

Fuel Strategy: Prioritize dense, slow-burning hardwoods. They require more effort to ignite, but the resulting embers burn longer and hotter, providing sustained warmth that is necessary to prevent hypothermia.

The Emergency Chemical and Found-Item Fire

In dire situations, you may need to rely on materials never intended for fire:

Chemical Starters: Certain common materials, like mixing Potassium Permanganate (a water purifier) with an accelerant like Glycerin (found in first-aid kits), create an intense exothermic reaction that results in immediate flame. This is hazardous and should only be used as a last resort.

Found Materials: Dry snack foods like corn chips (Fritos) or cotton pads soaked in lip balm/petroleum jelly make excellent, long-burning tinder due to their high fat or oil content. Even the wax on paper currency or wrappers can provide a critical few seconds of stable flame.

By mastering these troubleshooting techniques and environmental adaptations, you move beyond simply starting a fire to reliably managing fire in any condition. Now, you are ready to choose the perfect fire for any task.

Table 1: Global and Historical Origin of Ignition Methods

The precise origin date for friction methods is unknown, but archaeological evidence (like the tools Ötzi the Iceman carried) and ethnographic data give us strong indicators of their ancient and widespread use.

Ignition Method	Earliest Archaeological Evidence	Primary Global Usage
Percussion (Flint & Pyrite/Steel)	50,000 BCE (Pyrite/Marcasite) - Neanderthal tools, France; 3,300 BCE BCE (Ötzi's kit - Flint/Pyrite)	Widespread globally; became dominant in Europe, Asia, and the Arctic with the adoption of steel.
Hand Drill	Difficult to date; widespread evidence of its use among early human societies.	Arid, hot regions (e.g., North Africa, Australia, parts of North America).
Bow Drill	3,000 BCE (First evidence of rotary tools); widespread use in many ancient civilizations.	North America, Eurasia, and cultures needing higher efficiency than the hand drill.
Fire Plough	Used by ancient Austronesian and Polynesian cultures.	Primarily Southeast Asia and Pacific Islands.
Fire Saw/Thong	Difficult to date; relies on local plant materials (e.g., bamboo).	Tropical and South Pacific regions (e.g., Borneo, Philippines).
Fire Piston (Compression)	19th Century CE (Southeast Asia)	Indigenous cultures of Southeast Asia; later adopted as a niche modern survival tool.
Solar/Optical	As early as 3rd Century BCE (Myths of Archimedes using mirrors)	Ancient Greek and Roman temples; modern use with magnifying lenses.
Ferrocerium Rod	1903 CE (Invented by Auer von Welsbach)	Modern survival, camping, and military use.

Table 2: Global Usage of Fire Lays and Structures

This table connects your specialized structures to the environments or cultural regions that popularized them, reinforcing the "Advanced Natural Lays + Cultural Techniques" theme.

Fire Lay / Structure	Primary Cultural or Environmental Origin	Optimized Purpose
Teepee / Lean-To	Universal (Earliest, most intuitive structures)	Fast ignition, quick heat.
Log Cabin	European/North American Frontier/ Camping	Stable cooking platform, sustained burning.
Star Fire (Indian Lay)	North American Plains/ Indigenous Cultures	Maximum fuel conservation, minimal effort.
Dakota Fire Pit	Indigenous North American Plains Tribes	Stealth, high draft efficiency, wind resistance.
Swedish Torch (Log Candle)	Scandinavia/Northern Europe (Logging/ Military)	Contained heat/ light, temporary cooktop.
Keyhole Fire Pit	Camping/Outdoor Cooking Design	**Zone cooking**, advanced ember management.
Stone Boil / Mound Fire	Global Indigenous Cultures (Archaic)	Cooking without metal, minimum ground impact.
Rocket Stove / TLUD	Modern Appropriate Technology/Design	Extreme fuel efficiency, clean burning, biochar production.

Table 3: Wood Properties: Ignition and Burn Characteristics

This information is crucial **for replicability and efficiency, helping the reader select the best fuel for their needs. Generally, Softwoods are for starting (Kindling), and Hardwoods are for sustaining (Fuelwood).**

Wood Type (Example)	Category	Ignition Ease	Burn Temperature / Duration	Best Use
Cedar, Pine, Fir	**Softwood** (Resinous)	Easy (Due to high pitch/resin content)	Hot, Fast, Short Duration (High smoke output)	Excellent **Kindling** and fast-heating fire.
Basswood, Poplar, Willow	**Softwood** (Non-Resinous)	Medium	Medium-Fast (Low heat, little coaling)	Friction fire materials (Fireboard/Spindle).
Oak, Maple, Hickory	**Hardwood** (Dense)	Difficult (Requires sustained heat)	Very Hot, **Long Duration** (Excellent, long-lasting coals)	**Best for Warmth** (overnight) and coal cooking.
Ash, Birch	**Hardwood** (Medium Density)	Medium-Easy	Hot, Medium Duration (Birch bark is great tinder)	Good all-purpose fire and general cooking.

Table 4: Woods to Avoid: Toxic and Hazardous

The primary risk comes from wood that releases toxic compounds, irritants, or allergens when burned, and any wood that is preserved or treated.

1. Poisonous Trees (Do Not Burn)
These woods contain high concentrations of oils, resins, or toxic compounds that are aerosolized when burned, causing severe respiratory distress, allergic reactions, or poisoning.

Wood Type	Hazard	Risk When Burned
Pressure-Treated Wood	Chromated Copper Arsenate (CCA), various fungicides, and pesticides.	Releases arsenic and other heavy metals into the air and food. **Extremely poisonous.**
Plywood, Particle Board, MDF	Glues, resins (Urea-Formaldehyde, Phenol-Formaldehyde)	Releases toxic formaldehyde gas and other volatile organic compounds (VOCs).
Stained, Painted, or Finished Wood	Lead paint, petroleum distillates, solvents, and finishes.	Releases toxic vapors and heavy metal contaminants.
Pallet Wood	Often treated with hazardous fungicides/pesticides (look for the **"MB"** stamp indicating Methyl Bromide treatment).	Releases toxic fumes. Only use pallets marked **"HT"** (Heat Treated).

General Rule for Safety: If you cannot positively identify a wood, or if it has any chemical odor, do not burn it or use it for any food preparation. Stick to known, safe hardwoods like Oak, Maple, and Hickory for cooking coals.

Wood Type	Hazard	Risk When Burned
Poison Ivy, Poison Oak, Poison Sumac	Urushiol oil (highly toxic allergen)	Severe allergic reaction, rash, and blistering inside the lungs and airways.
Oleander	Highly toxic cardiac glycosides	Smoke is extremely poisonous; can be deadly if inhaled or if used for cooking.
Laburnum	Cytisine (highly toxic alkaloid)	Smoke is toxic; can cause vomiting, convulsions, and respiratory failure.
Yew (English Yew)	Taxine alkaloids (highly toxic)	All parts are toxic; smoke can cause dizziness, dilated pupils, and cardiac issues.
Rhododendron	Grayanotoxins	Smoke is toxic and can cause dizziness, low blood pressure, and cardiac issues.
Manchineel	Highly caustic sap/toxins	**Extremely dangerous**—smoke can cause temporary blindness and severe respiratory irritation (often called "the death apple tree").

General Rule for Safety: If you cannot positively identify a wood, or if it has any chemical odor, do not burn it or use it for any food preparation. Stick to known, safe hardwoods like Oak, Maple, and Hickory for cooking coals.

Table 5: Allergenic and Heavy Smoke Woods (Use with Caution)

These woods are generally not poisonous but are known to cause strong respiratory irritation or contain irritating compounds. Avoid sustained exposure to the smoke.

Wood Type	Irritant / Characteristic	Caution
Black Walnut	Juglone (mildly toxic and allergenic compound)	May cause severe allergic reaction in sensitive individuals; avoid cooking over it.
Eucalyptus	Volatile aromatic oils	Produces heavy soot and irritating smoke, especially in poorly ventilated areas.
Sassafras	Safrole (mild irritant)	Smoke can be irritating to the eyes and lungs; use sparingly.
Spruce/Pine (Green or Wet)	High resin and sap content	Produces heavy, acrid, black smoke and soot.

General Rule for Safety: If you cannot positively identify a wood, or if it has any chemical odor, do not burn it or use it for any food preparation. Stick to known, safe hardwoods like Oak, Maple, and Hickory for cooking coals.

Hazardous Materials and Waste to Never Burn

Table 6: Plastics and Foam

Plastics, regardless of type, release highly toxic compounds, heavy black smoke, and leave behind harmful residue.

Material	Hazard When Burned
All Plastics (bottles, bags, food wrappers, packaging)	Releases dioxins, furans, chlorine gas, and heavy metals (especially PVC), which are carcinogenic and severely toxic when inhaled.
Foam / Styrofoam	Releases styrene and benzene—potent neurotoxins and known carcinogens.
Rubber (tires, shoe soles, rubber bands)	Releases sulfur oxides, heavy metals, and oil residue, creating thick, toxic black smoke.

Table 7: Paper Products with Ink or Gloss (Caution)

Plain paper is fine, but many common paper products contain chemicals that become toxic when aerosolized.

Material	Hazard When Burned
Magazines, Glossy Paper, Catalogs	The brightly colored, glossy inks contain heavy metals (like lead and cadmium) which are released as toxic dust or smoke.
Colored Gift Wrap / Cardboard	Inks and dyes contain metallic compounds; colored smoke is a sign of toxic additives.
Cardboard with Tape or Wax Coating	Wax and glues (often petroleum-based) release irritating fumes and volatile organic compounds (VOCs).

Table 8: Food Scraps and Yard Waste

While non-toxic, these materials significantly impact the fire's quality and the environment.

Material	Hazard When Burned
Food Scraps / Garbage	Generates foul odors, attracts pests, and creates heavy, acrid smoke because of high moisture content.
Green / Freshly Cut Yard Waste	High moisture content wastes heat and creates excessive, polluting smoke (incomplete combustion).

Table 9: Flammable Liquids and Accelerants

Using any volatile liquid other than a tiny amount of natural accelerant (like pitch) is extremely dangerous.

Material	Hazard When Burned
Gasoline, Kerosene, Lighter Fluid	Highly explosive, creating sudden, unpredictable blasts of flame. Releases extremely irritating black smoke and hydrocarbon fumes.
Aerosol Cans (Empty or Full)	Pressurized cans can explode when heated, launching sharp metal fragments.

Table 10: Metal and Glass

These materials are pollutants that do not burn and can cause physical damage

Material	Hazard When Burned
Aluminum Cans, Tin Foil	Does not combust. Remains in the fire pit as pollution, wasting heat and energy.
Glass Bottles / Containers	Glass can melt and fuse with the fire pit floor, creating dangerous, sharp shards that ruin the area.

Final Rule: If it didn't grow naturally in the forest, and you can't eat it, assume it is toxic or hazardous and dispose of it properly in a sealed container for carry-out.

APPENDIX: COOKING WITH FIRE

Cooking on Embers (The Ideal Method)

Ember cooking means cooking over the bed of glowing red or white-hot coals left after the flame has died down. This is the best, most controllable heat source for camp cooking.

Characteristics of Ember Heat:

1. **Steady and Consistent:** Coals provide stable heat that lasts for a long time.

2. **Controllable:** Heat can be regulated by spreading or piling the coals (Keyhole Pit is ideal).

3. **Radiant:** Provides intense heat without the variable flare-ups of flame.

4. **Low Smoke:** Minimal smoke means less risk of acrid flavor or carcinogenic soot.

Food Item	Preparation Method	Why Embers Are Best
Steaks, Chops, Burgers	Place directly on a hot grill grate 3–5 inches above the coals.	Provides intense, even heat for perfect searing without scorching the exterior.
Roasting (Large Cuts)	Place in a Dutch oven or wrap heavily in foil and place beside the coals or bury under a thin layer.	Slow, consistent heat penetrates the center of roasts, chicken, or baked goods for thorough cooking.
Vegetables	Foil-wrapped or skewered; placed over or next to coals.	Prevents charring the delicate sugars in vegetables (onions, potatoes) while cooking them through.
Baking / Bread	Cooked in a cast-iron skillet or Dutch oven placed directly on or suspended above the coals.	Requires stable, moderate temperature to rise and brown evenly.
Boiling (Water/ Coffee)	Place a pot directly on a metal grate above tightly piled coals.	Coals provide concentrated, intense heat required for sustained boiling.

Cooking on Open Flame (The Quick Method)

Open flame cooking is cooking directly over the active flames. This method is fast but highly inconsistent, suitable for quick tasks and immediate heat.

Characteristics of Open Flame Heat:

1. **Inconsistent:** Temperatures fluctuate rapidly due to air movement and fresh fuel ignition.

2. **High Soot:** The visible flame, especially from Softwoods (pine, cedar), deposits heavy, black soot on pots and food.

3. **Searing/Scorching Risk:** The heat is concentrated and often too intense, leading to burnt exteriors and raw interiors.

Food Item	Preparation Method	Why Open Flame Is Best
Torching / Toasting	Hold food high above the flame on a long stick or skewer (e.g., marshmallows, hot dogs).	Utilizes the height and quick, direct heat for fast surface browning and cooking small items.
Pre-Boiling	Place a pot high above the flame, accepting the soot deposits.	Provides the quickest initial blast of heat to bring large volumes of water to a boil rapidly (e.g., heating water for dishes).
The Rocket Stove Method	Using a vessel on a Rocket Stove or Hobo Stove.	The stove structure harnesses the flame's energy for focused, intense heat, making this the only exception where flame cooking is highly efficient.
Bannock (on a stick)	Dough wrapped around a clean stick and held near the flame.	The radiant heat quickly bakes the thin dough layer.

www.ingramcontent.com/pod-product-compliance
Lightning Source LLC
Chambersburg PA
CBHW020755130626
46554CB00006B/2200